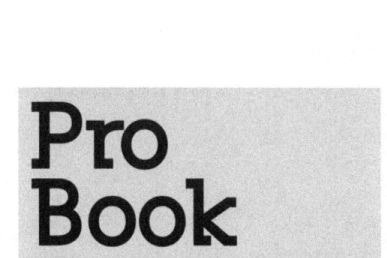

Pro Book

Adult COLORING COLORING *Book*

Stress relieving designs Stress relieving designs Stress relieving designs

animals collection

Let's Start ..

www.ingramcontent.com/pod-product-compliance
Lightning Source LLC
LaVergne TN
LVHW081541060225
803144LV00011B/380